Awesome to Absurd

Quotations to Guide Your Life...or Not

Jerry Cavanaugh

DEDICATION

To all my friends and family who have
made my life what it is.

Introduction

I have often found books of quotations to be tedious, boring, and not of much help when I am looking for inspiration, comfort, or some sense of direction in my life. Occasionally, however, I will come across a quotation that makes me think or smile. Those are the ones I have included in this book. They are definitely personal choices. There has been no attempt to include every important thing anyone has ever said or written. Bartlett has done that. These are words that touched something in me and, I hope, may touch the reader. If not, so be it.

The quotes are arranged alphabetically by the person credited with having spoken or written them. Where possible, I have included the appropriate dates of their lives. No particular reason, other than you might want to know.

Someone (I forget who) once said. "Any fool can write a book of quotations." This book is solid evidence of that. Nevertheless, I hope you enjoy it.

Jerry Cavanaugh

Note: All illustrations are by the author.

Jane Ace (1897-1974)

I think people who go to a psychiatrist ought to have their heads examined.

Lord Emerich Edward Dalberg Acton (First Baron Acton) (1834-1902)

Power tends to corrupt, and absolute power corrupts absolutely. Great men are almost always bad men...There is no worse heresy than that the office sanctifies the holder of it.

Liberty becomes a question of morals more than politics.

Everybody likes to get as much power as circumstances allow, and nobody will vote for a self-denying ordinance.

Official truth is not actual truth.

Americans dreaded democracy and contrived their constitution against it.

Progress, the religion of those who have none.

James Truslow Adams (1878-1949)

Slovenly language corrodes the mind.

Scott Adams (1957-   )

The children are our future. And that is why, ultimately, we're screwed unless we do something about it.

I think the only thing that keeps most people from randomly killing other citizens is the bloody mess it makes and the high likelihood of getting caught.

You can never underestimate the stupidity of the general public.

When it comes to physical toughness, there are two types of people: There are people like me...and then there are people who can beat the crap out of people like me.

Companies hire temp workers for much the same reasons that NASA used chimps in its early rocket testing.

Creativity is allowing yourself to make mistakes. Art is knowing which ones to keep.

Free will is an illusion. People always choose the perceived path of greatest pleasure.

People vote based on emotion. Period.

Aeschylus (c. 525-456 B.C.)

Memory is the mother of all wisdom.

Aesop (c. 620-564 B.C.)

Please all, and you will please none.

The gods help those who help themselves.

A liar will not be believed, even when he speaks the truth.

Do not count your chickens before they are hatched.

Familiarity breeds contempt.

After all is said and done, more is said than done.

Appearances are often deceiving.

The smaller the mind the greater the conceit.

Nelson Algren (1909-1981)

Never eat at a place called Mom's. Never play cards with a man called Doc. Never go to bed with a woman whose troubles are greater than your own.

Any writer who knows what he's doing isn't doing very much.

A certain ruthlessness and a sense of alienation from society is as essential to creative writing as it is to armed robbery.

Fred Allen (1894-1956)

A celebrity is a person who works hard all his life to become known, then wears dark glasses to avoid being recognized.

Woody Allen (1935-   )

You can live to be a hundred if you give up all the things that make you want to live to be a hundred.

Eighty percent of success is showing up.

If you want to make God laugh, tell him about your plans.

Harvard makes mistakes, too, you know. Kissinger taught there.

If you're not failing every now and again, it's a sign you're not doing anything very innovative.

Kingsley Amis (1922-1995)

Generally, nobody behaves decently when they have power.

If you can't annoy somebody, there is little point in writing.

It is no wonder that people are so horrible when they start life as children.

It is natural and harmless in English to use a preposition to end a sentence with.

Unquestioning devotion to authenticity is, in any department of life, a mark of the naïve – or worse.

Appius Claudius Caecus (c.340 -273 B.C.)

Each man is the architect of his own destiny.

Hannah Arendt (1906-1975)

Under conditions of tyranny it is far easier to act than to think.

The most radical revolutionary will become a conservative the day after the revolution.

This is the precept by which I have lived: Prepare for the worst, expect the best, and take what comes.

No punishment has ever possessed enough power of deterrence to prevent the commission of crimes.

Wisdom is a virtue of old age, and it seems to come only to those who, when young, were neither wise nor prudent.

Every generation, civilization is invaded by barbarians – we call them children.

Aristophanes (c. 446-386 B.C.)

Old age is a second childhood.

Under every stone lurks a politician.

Youth ages, immaturity is outgrown, ignorance can be educated, and drunkenness sobered, but stupid lasts forever.

The wise learn many things from their enemies.

You should not decide until you have heard what both have to say.

Aristotle (384-322 B.C.)

All men naturally desire knowledge.

Moral virtue is the child of habit.

Our actions determine our dispositions.

It is the mark of an educated mind to be able to entertain a thought without accepting it.

The only stable state is the one in which all men are equal before the law.

The secret of humor is surprise.

Margaret Atwood (1939-   )

An eye for an eye leads only to more blindness.

If you're not annoying somebody, you're not really alive.

I've never understood why people consider youth a time of freedom and joy. It's probably because they have forgotten their own.

If I waited for perfection...I would never write a word.

Another belief of mine: that everyone else my age is an adult, whereas I am merely in disguise.

War is what happens when language fails.

For years I wanted to be older, and now I am.

Francis Bacon (1561-1626)

Knowledge itself is power.

The great end of life is not knowledge but action.

A false friend is more dangerous than an open enemy.

Small matters win great commendation.

Money is like manure, not good except it be spread.

Opportunity makes a thief.

The root of all superstition is that men observe when a thing hits, but not when it misses.

There is no real use for wealth, but to give it to others.

Joan Baez (1941-   )

Action is the antidote to despair.

Walter Bagehot (1826-1877)

The great pleasure in life is doing what people say you cannot do.

James Baldwin (1924-1987)

Children have never been very good at listening to their elders, but they have never failed to imitate them.

Lucille Ball (1911-1989)

The secret to staying young is to live honestly, eat slowly, and lie about your age.

James M. Barrie (1860-1937)

Nothing is really work unless you would rather be doing something else.

I am not young enough to know everything.

Ethel Barrymore (1879-1959)

You grow up the day you have your first real laugh at yourself.

The best time to make friends is before you need them.

Bernard Baruch (1870-1965)

Every man has a right to be wrong in his opinions. But no man has a right to be wrong about his facts.

Sir Arnold Bax (1883-1953)

One should try everything once, except incest and folk-dancing.

Simone de Beauvoir (1908-1986)

If you live long enough, you'll find that every victory turns into a defeat.

Robert Benchley (1889-1945)

Anyone can do any amount of work, provided it isn't the work he is supposed to be doing at the moment.

The surest way to make a monkey of a man is to quote him.

Richard Benner (1943-1990)

Canada is a country so square than even the female impersonators are women.

Mary Frances Berry (1938-   )

The time when you need to do something is when no one else is willing to do it, when people are saying it can't be done.

Ambrose Bierce

(1842-c. 1914)

War is God's way of teaching Americans geography.

Doubt is the father of invention.

The small part of ignorance that we arrange and classify we give the name of knowledge.

To be positive is to be mistaken at the top of one's voice.

Success is the one unpardonable sin against our fellows.

Josh Billings (1818-1885)

If a man is right, he can't be too radical; if he is wrong, he can't be too conservative.

Prince Otto von Bismarck (1815-1898)

Politics is the doctrine of what is possible.

Lewis Black (1948-   )

There is nothing more obnoxious to an avid sports fan – okay, to me – than an athlete telling the audience after a big victory that God was the reason for it.

Religion is supposed to provide solace. Why, then, do so many people who practice religion end up killing themselves?

Sir William Blackstone (1723-1780)

It is better that ten guilty persons escape than one innocent suffer.

William Blake (1757-1827)

It is easier to forgive an Enemy than to forgive a Friend.

Man's desires are limited by his perceptions; none can desire what he has not perceived.

The weak in courage is strong in cunning.

What is now proved was once only imagined.

You never know what is enough unless you know what is more than enough.

Elayne Boosler (1952-   )

The Vatican is against surrogate mothers. Good thing they didn't have that rule when Jesus was born.

Kenneth Boulding (1910-1993)

Nothing fails like success because we don't learn from it. We learn only from failure.

Alec Bourne (1886-1974)

It is possible to store the mind with a million facts and still be entirely uneducated.

Georges Braque (1882-1963)

Art is meant to disturb.

Bertolt Brecht (1898-1956)

Feeding your face comes first, then morality.

Bank robbery is an initiative of amateurs. True professionals establish a bank.

Everyone needs help from everyone.

The aim of science is not to open the door to infinite wisdom, but to set a limit to infinite error.

No one can be good for long if goodness is not in demand.

David Brenner (1936-2014)

A vegetarian is a person who won't eat anything that can have children.

Kingman Brewster (1919-1988)

Incomprehensible jargon is the hallmark of a profession.

Marshall Brickman (1939-   )

When something good happens it's a miracle and you should wonder what God is saving up for you later.

John Bright (1811-1889)

Force is not a remedy.

Bob Brown (1944-   )

Behind every successful man there're a lot of unsuccessful years.

Thomas Edward Brown (1830-1897)

A rich man's joke is always funny.

William Jennings Bryan (1860-1925)

No one can earn a million dollars honestly.

Do not compute the totality of your poultry population until all the manifestations of incubation have been completed.

Edward George Bulwer-Lytton (1803-1873)

In science, read, by preference, the newest works; in literature, the oldest.

Talent does what it can; genius does what it must.

The pen is mightier than the sword.

The best teacher is the one who suggests rather than dogmatizes, and inspires his listener with the wish to teach himself.

The easiest person to deceive is one's self.

Luis Bunuel (1900-1983)

I am still an atheist, thank God.

Age is something that doesn't matter unless you're a cheese.

Life without memory is no life at all.

Edmund Burke (1729-1797)

No passion so effectually robs the mind of all its powers of acting and reasoning as fear.

It is a general popular error to imagine the loudest complainers for the public to be the most anxious for its welfare.

The march of the human mind is slow.

All government, indeed every human benefit and enjoyment, every virtue, and every prudent act, is founded on compromise and barter.

Liberty, too, must be limited in order to be possessed.

Superstition is the religion of feeble minds.

Our patience will achieve more than our force.

Example is the school of mankind, and they will learn at no other.

Religious persecution may shield itself under the guise of a mistaken and over-zealous piety.

The only thing necessary for the triumph of evil is for good men to do nothing.

George Burns (1896-1996)

Happiness is having a large, loving, caring, close-knit family in another city.

I honestly think it is better to be a failure at something you love than to be a success at something you hate.

The secret of a good sermon is to have a good beginning and a good ending, then having the two as close together as possible.

If you live to be a hundred, you've got it made. Very few people die past that age.

Someone who makes you laugh is a comedian. Someone who makes you think and then laugh is a humorist.

George H. W. Bush (1924-   )

People say I'm indecisive, but I don't know about that.

I put confidence in the American people, in their ability to sort through what is fair and what is unfair, what is ugly and what is unugly.

I will never apologize for the United States of America, ever. I don't care what the facts are.

It's no exaggeration to say that the undecideds could go one way or another.

I stand for anti-bigotry, anti-Semitism, and anti-racism.

George W. Bush (1946-   )

I think anybody who doesn't think I'm smart enough to handle the job is underestimating.

Presidents, whether things are good or bad, get the blame. I understand that.

The goals of this country is to enhance prosperity and peace.

Reading is the basics for all learning.

One of the great things about books is sometimes there are some fantastic pictures.

Families is where our nation finds hope, where wings take dream.

If you're sick and tired of the politics of cynicism and polls and principles, come and join this campaign.

I'm the master of low expectations.

More and more of our imports come from overseas.

The only way we can win is to leave before the job is done.

I know how hard it is for you to put food on your family.

I think we all agree, the past is over.

I hope that the ambitious realize they are more likely to succeed with success as opposed to failure

Nicholas Murray Butler (1862-1947)

An expert is one who knows more and more about less and less.

America is the best half-educated country in the world.

Many people's tombstones should read "Died at 30, buried at 60."

I divide the world into three classes – the few who make things happen, the many who watch things happen, the overwhelming majority who have no notion of what happens.

Cherish yesterday, dream tomorrow, live like crazy today!

Samuel Butler (1835-1902)

An honest God's the noblest work of man.

All progress is based upon a universal innate desire on the part of every organism to live beyond its income.

It costs a lot of money to die comfortably.

Parents are the last people on earth who ought to have children.

Brigands demand your money or your life; women require both.

Though wisdom cannot be gotten with gold, still less can it be gotten without it.

All of the animals, excepting man, know that the principal business of life is to enjoy it.

Life is one long process of getting tired.

James Branch Cabell (1879-1958)

The optimist proclaims that we live in the best of all possible worlds; the pessimist fears this is true.

Herb Caen (1916-1997)

The trouble with born-again Christians is that they are an even bigger pain the second time around.

Simon Cameron (1799-1889)

An honest politician is one who, when he is bought, will stay bought.

Albert Camus

(1913-1960)

Every revolutionary ends as an oppressor or a heretic.

Real generosity toward the future lies in giving all to the present.

Stupidity has a knack of getting its way.

It is a kind of spiritual snobbery that makes people think they can be happy without money.

Nobody realizes that some people expend tremendous energy merely to be normal.

No cause justifies the deaths of innocent people.

Don't wait for the last judgment – it takes place every day.

Alas, after a certain age every man is responsible for his face.

We are all special cases.

George Carlin (1937-2008)

Don't sweat the petty things and don't pet the sweaty things.

If it's true that our species is alone in the universe, then I'd have to say the universe aimed rather low and settled for very little.

Have you ever noticed? Anybody going slower than you is an idiot, and anyone going faster than you is a moron.

Ever wonder about those people who spend $2 apiece on those little bottles of Evian water? Try spelling Evian backward.

Think about how stupid the average person is, then realize that half the population is stupider.

Inside every cynical person there is a disappointed idealist.

Always do whatever's next.

Thomas Carlyle (1795-1881)

A great man shows his greatness by the way he treats little men.

Just in ratio as knowledge increases, faith diminishes

Thomas Carruthers (1839-1917)

A teacher is one who makes himself progressively unnecessary.

Miguel de Cervantes (1547-1616)

I say have patience, and shuffle the cards.

Tell me the company you keep, and I'll tell you who you are.

In order to attain the impossible, one must attempt the absurd.

No fathers or mothers think their own children ugly.

That which costs little is less valued.

Nicolas Chamfort (Sebastien-Roch Nicolas) (1741-1794)

Someone said of a great egotist: 'He would burn your house down to cook himself a couple of eggs.'

The only thing that stops God from sending another flood is that the first one was useless.

G.K. Chesterton (1874-1936)

The chief object of education is not to learn things but to unlearn things.

The rich are the scum of the earth in every country.

To be clever enough to get all that money, one must be stupid enough to want it.

It's not the world that's got so much worse but the news coverage that's got so much better.

The Christian ideal, it is said, has not been tried and found wanting: it has been found difficult and left untried.

Art, like morality, consists of drawing the line somewhere.

The way to love anything is to realize that it may be lost.

When it comes to life the critical thing is whether you take things for granted or take them with gratitude.

How you think when you lose determines how long it will be until you win.

It is the test of a good religion whether you can joke about it.

Maurice Chevalier (1888-1972)

Many a man has fallen in love with a girl in a light so dim he would not choose a suit by it.

Sir Winston Churchill (1874-1965)

It is a good thing for an uneducated man to read books of quotations.

Success is walking from failure to failure with no loss of enthusiasm.

Never hold discussions with the monkey when the organ grinder is in the room.

If you are going through hell, keep going.

The best argument against democracy is a five-minute conversation with the average voter.

You can always count on Americans to do the right thing – after they've tried everything else.

Marcus Tullius Cicero (106-43 B.C.)

But somehow there is nothing so absurd that some philosopher has not said it.

The good of the people is the chief law.

Tom Clancy (1947-2013)

The difference between fiction and reality? Fiction has to make sense.

Eldridge Cleaver (1935-1998)

If you are not part of the answer, you are part of the problem.

Georges Clemenceau (1841-1929)

It is easier to make war than to make peace.

America is the only nation in history which miraculously has gone directly from barbarism to degeneration without the usual interval of civilization.

Peter Cocotas

One good thing about being a man is that men don't have to talk to each other.

Stanley N. Cohen (1935-   )

Nature is that lovely lady to whom we owe polio, leprosy, smallpox, syphilis, tuberculosis, and cancer.

John Churton Collins (1848-1908)

A fool often fails because he thinks what is difficult is easy.

Mortimer Collins (1827-1876)

A man is as old as he's feeling, a woman as old as she looks.

Charles Caleb Colton (c. 1780-1832)

When you have nothing to say, say nothing.

Imitation is the sincerest form of flattery.

Auguste Comte (1798-1857)

The universe displays no proof of an all-directing mind.

Richard Condon (1915-1996

Writers are too self-centered to be lonely.

Confucius (551-479 B.C.)

Real knowledge is to know the extent of one's own ignorance.

What you do not want done to yourself, do not do to others.

Study the past, if you would divine the future.

Sir William Congreve (1772-1828)

There is good in seeing good in others.

Cyril Connolly (1903-1974)

Whom the gods wish to destroy they first call promising.

Better to write for yourself and have no public, than write for the public and have no self.

Always be nice to those younger than you, because they are the ones who will be writing about you.

James Connolly (1868-1916)

Governments in a capitalist society are but committees of the rich to manage the affairs of the capitalist class.

Joseph Conrad (1857-1924)

The terrorist and the policeman both come from the same basket.

Sir Noel Coward (1899-1973)

Work is much more fun than fun.

We have no reliable guarantee that the afterlife will be any less exasperating than this one, have we?

William Cowper (1731-1800)

A fool must now and then be right, by chance.

Bishop Richard Cumberland (1631-1718)

It is better to wear out than to rust out.

Frank Dane

Life is strange. Every so often a good man wins.

Clarence Darrow (1857-1938)

I don't believe in God because I don't believe in Mother Goose.

Sir Humphrey Davy (1778-1829)

The most important of my discoveries have been suggested to me by my failures.

James Dean (1931-1955)

Dream as if you'll live forever. Live as if you'll die today.

Daniel Defoe (1660-1731)

Necessity makes an honest man a knave.

The best of men cannot suspend their fate: The good die early, and the bad die late...

Wherever God erects a house of prayer,

The Devil always builds a chapel there;

And will be found upon examination,

The latter has the largest congregation.

Edgar Degas (1834-1917)

Painting is easy when you don't know how, but very difficult when you do.

Charles DeGaulle (1890-1970)

The graveyards are full of indispensable men.

Willem de Kooning (1904-1997)

The trouble with being poor is that it takes up all your time.

Philippe Nericault Destouches (1680-1754)

The absent are always in the wrong.

Peter De Vries (1910-1993)

We know the human brain is a device to keep the ears from grating on one another.

It is the final proof of God's omnipotence that he need not exist in order to save us.

John Dewey (1859-1952)

To find out what one is fitted to do and to secure an opportunity to do it is the key to happiness.

Charles Dickens (1812-1870)

No one is useless in this world who lightens the burden of it to anyone else.

Denis Diderot (1713-1784)

All children are essentially criminal.

Marlene Dietrich (c. 1904-1992)

If there is a supreme being, he's crazy.

Everett Dirksen (1896-1969)

I am a man of fixed and unbending principles, the first of which is to be flexible at all times.

Norman Douglas (1868-1952)

You can tell the ideals of a nation by its advertisements.

Marie Dressler (1869-1934)

If ants are such busy workers, how come they find time to go to all the picnics?

John Dryden (1631-1700)

Beware the fury of a patient man.

Alexandre Dumas (Fils) (1824-1895)

If God were suddenly condemned to live the life which he had inflicted on men, He would kill Himself.

All generalizations are dangerous, even this one.

Will Durant (1885-1981)

Education is a progressive discovery of our own ignorance.

Bob Dylan (1941-   )

Just because you like my stuff, doesn't mean I owe you anything.

Roger Ebert (1942-2013)

What you do instead of your work is your real work.

Mary Baker Eddy (1821-1910)

Health is not a condition of matter, but of Mind.

Thomas Edison (1847-1931)

If we did all the things we are capable of doing, we would literally astonish ourselves.

Bob Edwards (1947-   )

One trouble with being efficient is that it makes everybody hate you so.

Albert Einstein (1879-1955)

Imagination is more important than knowledge.

The difference between stupidity and genius is that genius has its limits.

Once you can accept the universe as being something expanding into an infinite nothing which is something, wearing stripes with plaid is easy.

If the idea is not at first absurd, then there is no hope for it.

The definition of insanity is doing the same thing over and over again and expecting different results.

Only two things are infinite – the universe and human stupidity, and I'm not sure about the universe.

Common sense is the collection of prejudices acquired by age eighteen.

The only good life is the one that is lived for others.

George Eliot (Mary Ann Evans) (1819-1880)

What do we live for, if it is not to make life less difficult for each other?

Nothing is so good as it seems beforehand.

An election is coming. Universal peace is declared, and the foxes have a sincere interest in prolonging the lives of the poultry.

I'm not denyin' the women are foolish: God Almighty made 'em to match the men.

Conscientious people are apt to see their duty in that which is the most painful course.

Duke Ellington (1899-1974)

A problem is a chance for you to do your best.

Harlan Ellison (1934-   )

The two most abundant things in the universe are hydrogen and stupidity.

Ralph Waldo Emerson (1803-1882)

Nothing great was ever achieved without enthusiasm.

Nothing astonishes men so much as common sense and plain dealing.

The reward of a thing well done, is to have done it.

The way to have friends is to be one.

No change of circumstance can repair a defect of character.

Win as if you were used to it, lose as if you enjoyed it for a change.

A hero is no braver than an ordinary man, but he is braver five minutes longer.

Fame is proof that the people are gullible.

Quintus Ennius (c. 239-169 B.C.)

They hate whom they fear.

Desiderius Erasmus (1466-1536)

It is well known, that among the blind the one-eyed man is king.

War is sweet to those who have not tried it.

Sven-Goran Eriksson (1948-   )

The greatest barrier to success is the fear of failure.

Edward M. Esber (1952-   )

A computer will not make a good manager out of a bad manager. It makes a good manager better faster and a bad manager worse faster.

Dame Edith Evans (1888-1976)

When a woman behaves like a man, why doesn't she behave like a nice man?

Fabaria

Men do more things from custom than from reason.

Jean de la Fontaine (1621-1695)

A hungry stomach will not listen.

Henry Ford (1863-1947)

Failure is simply the opportunity to begin again, this time more intelligently.

Whether you think you can or think you can't, you're right.

Quality means doing it right when no one is looking.

Luke Ford (1966-   )

Everything we do affects other people.

Benjamin Franklin (1706-1790)

Creditors have better memories than debtors.

There are more old drunkards than old doctors.

Experience is the worst teacher. It always gives the test first and the instruction afterward.

James Anthony Froude (1818-1894)

Fear is the parent of cruelty.

Wild animals never kill for sport. Man is the only one to whom the torture and death of his fellow creatures is amusing in itself.

(Sarah) Margaret Fuller (1810-1850)

I made up my mind to be bright and ugly.

I now know all the people worth knowing in America, and I find no intellect comparable to my own.

There is no modesty or moderation in me.

R. Buckminster Fuller (1895-1983)

I look for what needs to be done. After all, that's how the universe designs itself.

Paul Fussell (1924-2012)

I find nothing more depressing than optimism.

John Kenneth Galbraith (1908-2006)

When people are least sure they are most dogmatic.

Indira Gandhi (1917-1984)

You cannot shake hands with a clenched fist.

There exists no politician in India daring enough to attempt to explain to the masses that cows can be eaten.

Gabriel Garcia-Marquez (1927-2014)

There are no limits to human ingratitude.

One single minute of reconciliation is worth more than an entire life of friendship.

Althea Gibson (1927-2003)

No matter what accomplishments you make, somebody helps you.

William Schwenck Gilbert (1836-1911)

Things are seldom what they seem,

Skim milk masquerades as cream.

I see no objection to stoutness, in moderation.

Brendan Gill (1914-1997)

Not a shred of evidence exists in favor of the idea that life is serious.

Gail Godwin (1937-   )

Good teaching is one-quarter preparation and three-quarters theater.

Johann Wolfgang von Goethe (1749-1832)

There is nothing in which people more betray their character than in what they laugh at.

Oliver Goldsmith (1728-1774)

Every absurdity has a champion to defend it.

George Gordon, Lord Byron (1788-1824)

If I could always read, I should never feel the want of society.

Always laugh when you can. It is cheap medicine.

What a strange thing man is; and what a stranger thing woman.

Truth is always strange, stranger than fiction.

A celebrity is one who is known to many persons he is glad he doesn't know.

Victor Grayson (1881-1920)

Never explain: your friends don't need it and your enemies won't believe it.

Thomas Hardy (1840-1928)

If Galileo had said in verse that the world moved, the Inquisition might have let him alone.

Though a good deal is too strange to be believed, nothing is too strange to have happened.

Sydney J. Harris (1917-1986)

Our dilemma is that we hate change and love it at the same time; what we really want is for things to remain the same but get better.

Orrin Hatch (1934-   )

Capital punishment is our society's recognition of the sanctity of human life.

Roy Hattersley (1932-   )

Familiarity with evil breeds not contempt but acceptance.

William Hazlitt (1778-1830)

A nickname is the heaviest stone that the devil can throw at a man.

Violent antipathies are always suspicious, and betray a secret affinity.

No young man believes he shall ever die.

The least pain in our little finger gives us more concern and uneasiness, than the destruction of millions of our fellow beings.

Learning is its own exceeding great reward.

Heraclitus (c. 535-c. 475 B.C.)

You cannot step twice into the same river.

John Hervey, 2nd Baron Hervey (1696-1743)

Whoever would lie usefully should lie seldom.

Joel Hildebrand (1881-1983)

Very few people do anything creative after the age of thirty-five. The reason is that very few people do anything creative before the age of thirty-five.

Napoleon Hill (1883-1970)

It is always your next move.

Don't wait. The time will never be just right.

Reginald Hill (1936-2012)

I have seen the future and it sucks.

The first thing revolutionaries of the left or right give up is their sense of humor. The second thing is other people's rights.

Eric Hoffer (1898-1983)

When people are free to do as they please, they usually imitate each other.

Passionate hatred can give meaning and purpose to an empty life.

Where there is the necessary technical skill to move mountains, there is no need for the faith that moves mountains

There would be no society if living together depended upon understanding each other.

Oliver Wendell Holmes, Jr. (1841-1935)

All life is experiment.

Richard Hooker (1554-1600)

Change is not made without inconvenience, even from worse to better.

Herbert Hoover (1874-1964)

When a great many people are unable to find work, unemployment results.

About the time we think we can make ends meet, somebody moves the ends.

Horace (65-8 B.C.)

Nothing is perfect from every point of view.

To have made a beginning is half of the business; dare to be wise.

Believe every day that has dawned is your last.

Donald Richmond Horne (1921-2005)

Politicians cannot help being clowns. Political activity is essentially absurd.

Edgar Watson Howe (1853-1937)

None of us can boast about the morality of our ancestors. The records do not show that Adam and Eve were married.

Elbert Hubbard (1856-1915)

The object of teaching a child is to enable him to get along without his teacher.

Life is just one damned thing after another.

Little minds are interested in the extraordinary; great minds in the commonplace.

The supernatural is the natural not yet understood.

A failure is a man who has blundered but is not able to cash in the experience.

A conservative is a man who is too cowardly to fight and too fat to run.

To escape criticism – do nothing, say nothing, be nothing.

The graveyards are full of people the world could not do without.

The love we give away is the only love we keep.

Kin Hubbard (1868-1930)

The hardest thing is writing a recommendation for someone we know.

Charles Evans Hughes (1862-1948)

When we lose the right to be different, we lose the privilege to be free.

Victor Hugo (1802-1885)

For the word is the Verb, and the Verb is God.

Francis Hutcheson (1694-1746)

That action is best, which procures the greatest happiness for the greatest numbers.

Robert Maynard Hutchins (1899-1977)

The object of education is to prepare the young to educate themselves throughout their lives.

Aldous Huxley (1894-1963)

That men do not learn very much from the lessons of history is the most important of all the lessons that history has to teach.

Several excuses are always less convincing than one.

Facts do not cease to exist because they are ignored.

Parodies and caricatures are the most penetrating criticisms.

Most human beings have an almost infinite capacity for taking things for granted.

The vast majority of human beings are not interested in reason or satisfied with what it teaches.

Maybe this world is another planet's Hell.

Science has "explained" nothing; the more we know, the more fantastic the world becomes and the profounder the surrounding darkness.

An intellectual is a person who has discovered something more interesting than sex.

Ye shall know the truth, and the truth shall make you mad as hell.

Ignore death up to the last moment; then, when it can't be ignored any longer, have yourself squirted full of morphine and shuffle off in a coma. Thoroughly sensible, humane, and scientific, eh?

Every man's memory is his private literature.

Thomas Henry Huxley (1825-1895)

Try to learn something about everything and everything about something.

There are some people who see a great deal and some who see very little in the same things.

Dolores Ibarruri (1895-1989)

It is better to die on your feet than to live on your knees.

It is better to be the widow of a hero than the wife of a coward.

Henrik Ibsen (1828-1906)

Fools are in a terrible, overwhelming majority, all the wide world over.

Robert Green Ingersoll (1833-1899)

In nature there are neither rewards nor punishments – there are consequences.

Robert Jackson (US Attorney General) (1892-1954)

The price of freedom of religion is that we must put up with a lot of rubbish.

William James (1842-1910)

The deepest principle in human nature is the craving to be appreciated.

The art of being wise is the art of knowing what to overlook.

Thomas Jefferson (1743-1826)

I have recently been examining all the known superstitions of the world, and do not find in our particular superstition (Christianity) one redeeming feature. They are all alike founded on fables and mythology.

Jerome K. Jerome (1859-1927)

It is impossible to enjoy idling thoroughly unless one has plenty of work to do.

I like work; it fascinates me. I can sit and look at it for hours. I love to keep it by me: the idea of getting rid of it nearly breaks my heart.

Douglas Jerrold (1803-1857)

If I were a gravedigger or even a hangman, there are some people I could work for with a great deal of enjoyment.

Samuel Johnson (1709-1784)

Patriotism is the last refuge of a scoundrel.

No man but a blockhead ever wrote, except for money.

Hell is paved with good intentions

A decent provision for the poor is the true test of civilization.

Nothing will ever be attempted if all possible objections must be first overcome.

Erica Jong (1942-   )

Advice is what we ask for when we already know the answer but wish we didn't.

Janis Joplin (1943-1970)

Don't compromise yourself. You are all you've got.

Joseph Joubert (1754-1824)

Children need models rather than critics.

To teach is to learn twice.

The Judge Magazine, 1927

The average person thinks he isn't.

Carl Jung (1875-1961)

Man needs difficulties; they are necessary for health.

Jean-Baptist Alphonse Karr (1808-1890)

The more things change; the more they remain the same.

John F. Kennedy (1917-1963)

The time to repair the roof is when the sun is shining.

Johannes Kepler (1571-1630)

Nature uses as little as possible of anything.

Ellen Key (1849-1926)

Corporal punishment is as humiliating for him who gives it as for him who receives it, it is ineffective besides. Neither shame nor physical pain have any other effect than a hardening one.

Ayatollah Khomeini (1900-1989)

An Islamic regime must be serious in every field. There are no jokes in Islam. There is no humor in Islam. There is no fun in Islam.

Soren Kierkegaard (1813-1855)

Life can only be understood backwards; but it must be lived forwards.

Florence King (1936-2016)

The more immoral we become in big ways, the more puritanical we become in little ways.

Martin Luther King, Jr. (1929-1968)

Nothing pains some people more than having to think.

Ed Koch (1924-2013)

Life is indeed precious. And I believe the death penalty helps to affirm the fact.

Irving Kristol (1920-2009)

Democracy does not guarantee equality of conditions. It only guarantees equality of opportunity.

Fran Lebowitz (1950-   )

All God's children are not beautiful. Most of God's children are, in fact, barely presentable.

Barry LePatner (1947-   )

Good judgment comes from experience and experience comes from bad judgment.

Claude Levi-Strauss (1908-2009)

The wise man is not the man who gives the right answers; he is the one who asks the right questions.

Roger Lewin (1944-   )

Too often we give children answers to remember rather than problems to solve.

Sinclair Lewis (1885-1951)

People will buy anything that's one to a customer.

Gerald F. Lieberman (1923-1986)

Freedom of the press is useless when people do not understand what they read.

Norman Lindsay (1879-1969)

The best love affairs are those we never had.

David Lloyd-George (1863-1945)

Love your neighbor is not merely sound Christianity; it is good business.

Alice Roosevelt Longworth (1884-1980)

I've always believed in the adage that the secret of eternal youth is arrested development.

Richard Lovelace (1618-1657)

Stone walls do not a prison make, nor iron bars a cage.

Luc de Clapiers, Marquis de Vauvenargues (1715-1747)

To achieve great things, we must live as though we are never going to die.

Martin Luther (1483-1546)

Reason is the enemy of faith.

Thomas Babington Macauley (1800-1859)

Perhaps no person can be a poet, or can even enjoy poetry, without a certain unsoundness of mind.

Lester Maddox (1915-2003)

Why would we have different races if God meant us to be alike and associate with each other?

James Magary

Computers can figure out all kinds of problems, except the things in the world that just don't add up.

Horace Mann (1796-1859)

If it were in my power, I would scatter books broadcast over the land, as the sower scatters grain in the furrows of the field.

It is a great mistake to be a slave to books. The secret of education is not love of books, but love of knowledge.

Build schools then; you will thus abolish ignorance, crime, and misery. You will quench hatred and make the happiness and greatness of the nation through the prosperity and morality of each of its citizens.

If a mob collects anywhere, instead of reading the riot act to disperse it, one has only to announce a lecture on education; that will be sufficient – not a soul will remain.

Whence comes it that one-quarter of the children who came into the world die before reaching the age of one year, unless it results from general ignorance of the laws of life.

How many dead minds there are to resuscitate!

There is no treasure comparable to truth; there is no such source of happiness as truth; there is no cure for misfortune like truth...

In fact, if we allow the character and talents of school-teachers to be lowered, the schools will become poor, and poor schools will form poor minds, and the free press will become a lying and licentious press, and the ignorant elector will become a venal elector until, under the outward form of a republic, a set of depraved and criminal men will govern the country.

He who does the most good to his fellow-men is the master of masters and has learned the art of arts.

It would be easier to turn back the sun in his course than to monopolize again in the hands of a few people the power which has passed into the hands of the people. Sooner will the oak reenter the acorn than we shall return to the monarchical and aristocratic forms of the past.

Ideas of liberty, duty, and fraternity now move the nations, and neither the Pope with his Cardinals nor the Czar with his Cossacks will succeed in suppressing them

It is perhaps easy to found a republic; it certainly is not easy to make republicans.

Education is our only political safeguard; outside of this ark there is no salvation.

For a teacher to succeed he must have won the affection of his pupils. The child will learn nothing, not even mathematics, from a teacher he does not like.

No punishment is beneficent except on condition of its being more painful to him who inflicts than to him who undergoes it.

Jean Paul Marat (1743-1793)

God has always been hard on the poor.

Marcus Aurelius (121-180)

And you will give yourself peace if you perform each act as if it were your last.

The art of living is more like wrestling than dancing.

The only wealth which you will keep forever is the wealth you have given away.

How much time he saves who does not look to see what his neighbor says or does or thinks.

Reject your sense of injury and the injury itself disappears.

Our life is what our thoughts make it.

Don Marquis (1878-1937)

The successful people are the ones who can think up things for the rest of the world to keep busy at.

Groucho Marx (1891-1961)

Many years ago I chased a woman for almost two years, only to discover her tastes were exactly like mine: we were both crazy about girls.

Tom Masson (1866-1934)

"Be yourself" is about the worst advice you can give to people.

Andrew W. Mathis

It is bad luck to be superstitious.

William Somerset Maugham (1874-1965)

People ask you for criticism, but they only want praise.

Impropriety is the soul of wit.

Life is too short to do anything for oneself that one can pay others to do for one.

Elsa Maxwell (1883-1963)

Laugh at yourself first, before anyone else can.

Mary McGrory (1918-2004)

Baseball is what we were, football is what we have become.

Mignon McLaughlin (1913-1983)

Most of us become parents long before we have stopped being children.

No one really listens to anyone else, and if you try it for a while you'll see why.

Marshall McLuhan (1911-1980)

If the nineteenth century was the age of the editorial chair, ours is the century of the psychiatrist's couch.

Ads are the cave art of the twentieth century.

The name of a man is a numbing blow from which he never recovers.

Margaret Mead (1901-1978)

Always remember that you are absolutely unique. Just like everyone else.

Every time we liberate a woman, we liberate a man.

Herman Melville (1819-1891)

I cherish the greatest respect towards everybody's religious obligations, never mind how comical.

H.L. Mencken (1880-1956)

There is always an easy solution to every human problem – neat, plausible, and wrong.

Don't overestimate the decency of the human race.

On some great and glorious day the plain folks of the land will reach their heart's desire at last, and the White House will be adorned by a downright moron.

Conscience is the inner voice that warns us somebody may be looking.

Bachelors have consciences, married men have wives.

On one issue at least, men and women agree; they both distrust women.

We must respect the other fellow's religion, but only in the sense and to the extent that we respect his theory that his wife is beautiful and his children smart.

The urge to save humanity is almost always a false front for the urge to rule.

The biggest hoax perpetrated by the human mind is its "life after death" valentine.

Marvin Minsky (1927-2016)

Logic doesn't apply to the real world.

Wilson Mizner (1876-1933)

I respect faith, but doubt is what gets you an education.

Walter Mondale (1928-   )

If you are sure you understand everything that is going on around you, you are hopelessly confused.

Ashley Montagu (1905-1999)

I want to die young at a ripe old age.

George Moore (1852-1933)

The wrong way always seems the more reasonable.

Alberto Moravia (1907-1990)

Nowadays the illiterates can read and write.

Hannah More (1745-1833)

In men this blunder still you find,

All think their little set mankind.

Dwight Morrow (1873-1931)

The world is divided into people who do things and people who get the credit.

Benito Mussolini (1883-1945)

The history of saints is mainly the history of insane people.

Gerald Nachman (1938-   )

The toughest part of being on a diet is shutting up about it.

Ogden Nash (1902-1971)

People who work sitting down get paid more than people who work standing up.

Paul Newman (1925-2008)

Show me a good loser and I'll show you a loser.

Sir Isaac Newton (1642-1727)

If I have seen further it is by standing on the shoulders of giants.

Friedrich Nietzsche (1844-1900)

That which doesn't kill us makes us stronger.

Is man one of God's blunders, or is God one of man's blunders?

Gregory Nunn (1955-   )

A conservative is a man who wants the rules changed so that no one can make a pile the way he did.

Michael O'Donoghue (1940-1994)

Life is not for everyone.

Victor O'Reilly (1944-   )

If at first you don't succeed, well, so much for skydiving.

P.J. O'Rourke (1947-   )

Everybody wants to save the earth; nobody wants to help Mom do the dishes.

The only thing that can be safely said about the great majority of people is that we don't want them around.

George Orwell (Eric Arthur Blair) (1903-1950)

Whatever is funny is subversive, every joke is ultimately a custard pie...a dirty joke is not...a serious attack upon morality, but it is a sort of mental rebellion, a momentary wish that things were otherwise.

At 50, everyone has the face he deserves.

On the whole, human beings want to be good, but not too good, and not quite all the time.

Ross Papprill

There are two kinds of people in the world: those who believe there are two kinds of people in the world, and those who don't.

Dorothy Parker (1893-1967)

Beauty is only skin deep, but ugly goes clean to the bone.

The cure for boredom is curiosity. There is no cure for curiosity.

Linus Pauling (1901-1994)

The best way to have a good idea is to have lots of ideas.

Laurence J. Peter (1919-1990)

A pessimist is a man who looks both ways before crossing a one-way street.

Middle age is when anything new in the way you feel is most likely a symptom.

In a hierarchy every employee tends to rise to his level of incompetence.

Work is accomplished by those employees who have not yet reached their level of incompetence.

Speak when you are angry – and you'll make the best speech you'll ever regret.

Some problems are so complex that you have to be highly intelligent and well informed just to be undecided about them.

E.J. Phelps (1822-1900)

The man who makes no mistakes does not usually make anything.

Pablo Picasso (1881-1973)

God is really only another artist. He invented the giraffe, the elephant, and the cat. He has no real style, he just goes on trying other things.

Plato (c. 428-347 B.C.)

He was a wise man who invented God.

Edgar Allan Poe (1809-1849)

The best place to hide anything is in plain view.

Pope Leo XIII (1810-1903)

The equal toleration of all religions...is the same thing as atheism.

Owens Lee Pomeroy (1929-2008)

Nostalgia is like a grammar lesson: you find the present tense, but the past perfect.

Sir Karl Popper (1902-1994)

It is impossible to speak in such a way that you cannot be misunderstood.

A. L. Prusick (1941-2008)

It may be that we have all lived before and died, and this is hell.

Publilius Syrus (85 -43 B.C.)

To do two things at once is to do neither.

Roy Qualley

If it tastes good, it's trying to kill you.

Dan Quayle (1947-   )

I believe we are on an irreversible trend toward more freedom and democracy. But that could change.

Francois Rabelais (1494-1553)

Nature abhors a vacuum.

Ayn Rand (1905-1982)

A creative man is motivated by the desire to achieve, not by the desire to beat others.

Jeanette Rankin (1880-1973)

You can no more win a war than you can win an earthquake.

Ronald Reagan (1911-2004)

What would this country be, without this great land of ours?

The State of California has no business subsidizing intellectual curiosity.

Ambrose Redmoon (James Neil Hollingworth) (1933-1996)

Courage is not the absence of fear, but rather the judgment that something else is more important than fear.

Joe Restivo (1952-2007)

Never ask old people how they are if you have anything else to do that day.

Rochefoucauld, Francois, Duc de la (1613-1680)

We are all strong enough to bear the sufferings of others.

Greater virtues are needed to sustain good fortune than bad.

One gives nothing so generously as advice.

Intellectual blemishes, like facial ones, grow more prominent with age.

Will Rogers (1879-1935)

Everything is funny as long as it happens to someone else.

When you put down the good things you ought to have done, and leave out the bad things you did do – that's Memoirs.

Madame Roland (1754-1793)

There is an intimate alliance between genius and insanity.

Charles Victor Roman (1864-1934)

No human folly can suppress the conceit of ignorance.

Eleanor Roosevelt (1884-1962)

No one can make you feel inferior without your consent.

You must do the thing you think you cannot do.

Jean-Jacques Rousseau (1712-1778)

One is only curious in proportion to one's level of education.

Rita Rudner (1953-   )

Human nature is largely something that has to be overcome.

Some people get so rich, they lose all respect for humanity. That's how rich I want to be.

David Ruggles (1810-1849)

Prejudice is not so much dependent upon natural antipathy as upon education.

John Ruskin (1819-1900)

It is far more difficult to be simple than to be complicated.

Bertrand Russell (1872-1970)

No one gossips about other people's secret virtues.

Many people would rather die than think. In fact, they do.

Few people can be happy unless they hate some other person, nation, or creed.

Patriots always talk of dying for their country, and never of killing for their country.

The fact that an opinion has been widely held is no evidence whatever that it is not utterly absurd; indeed, in view of the silliness of the majority of mankind, a widespread belief is more likely to be foolish than sensible.

So far as I can remember, there is not one word in the Gospels in praise of intelligence.

Patriotism is the willingness to kill and be killed for trivial reasons.

One of the symptoms of an approaching nervous breakdown is the belief that one's work is terribly important.

Anything you're good at contributes to happiness.

Saki (Hector Hugh Munro) (1870-1916)

Women and elephants never forget an injury.

But, good gracious, you've got to educate him first. You can't expect a boy to be vicious till he's been to a good school.

Herbert Samuel (1870-1963)

An autobiography is the story of how a man thinks he lived.

Margaret Sanger (1883-1966)

No woman can call herself free who does not own and control her own body.

George Santayana (1863-1952)

Almost every wise saying has an opposite one, no less wise, to balance it.

May Sarton (1912-1995)

Loneliness is the poverty of self; solitude is the richness of self.

A garden is always a series of losses set against a few triumphs, like life itself.

Diane Sawyer (1945-   )

I think the one lesson I have learned is that there is no substitute for paying attention.

Pete Seeger (1919-2014)

Education is when you read the fine print. Experience is what you get if you don't.

Seneca (c. 5 B.C. – 65 A.D.)

Fidelity bought with money can be overcome by money.

There is no great genius free from some tincture of madness.

Anne Sexton (1928-1974)

It doesn't matter who my father was; it matters who I remember he was.

Thomas Shadwell (c. 1642-1692)

Every man loves what he is good at.

Ronnie Shakes (1947-1987)

I like life. It's something to do.

George Bernard Shaw (1856-1950)

We don't stop playing because we grow old; we grow old because we stop playing.

I believe in the discipline of silence and could talk for hours about it.

There is only one universal passion: fear.

We learn from experience that men never learn anything from experience.

People get tired of everything, and of nothing sooner than of what they most like.

There are two tragedies in life. One is to lose your heart's desire. The other is to gain it.

The lesson intended by an author is hardly ever the lesson the world chooses to learn from his book.

Why should we take advice on sex from the Pope? If he knows anything about it, he shouldn't.

There is no satisfaction in hanging a man who does not object to it.

He knows nothing; and he thinks he knows everything. That points clearly to a political career.

It's all that the young can do for the old, to shock them and keep them up to date.

Assassination is the extreme form of censorship.

All great truths begin as blasphemies.

Progress is impossible without change, and those who cannot change their minds cannot change anything.

If you cannot get rid of the family skeleton, you may as well make it dance.

The average person today is about as credulous as was the average person in the Middle Ages.

There is only one religion, though there are a hundred versions of it.

A mind the caliber of mine cannot derive its nutriment from cows.

Whiskey is liquid sunshine.

A gentleman is one who puts more into the world than he takes out.

Liberty means responsibility; that is why most men dread it.

If you must hold yourself up to your children, hold yourself up as an object lesson and not as an example.

The golden rule is that there are no golden rules.

Patriotism is your conviction that this country is superior to all other countries because you were born in it.

Somebody must get the incompetent lawyers and doctors.

Even the youngest of us may be wrong sometimes.

Isaac Bashevis Singer (1904-1991)

We have to believe in free will. We've got no choice.

Dame Edith Sitwell (1887-1964)

I am patient with stupidity, but not with those who are proud of it.

Red Skelton (1913-1997)

All men make mistakes, but married men find out about them sooner.

Cornelia Otis Skinner (1899-1979)

Woman's virtue is man's greatest invention.

Philip Slater (1927-2013)

Every American thinks he's alone on the continent.

Alfred E. Smith (1873-1944)

Without the help of thousands of others, any one of us would die, naked and starved.

Stevie Smith (Florence Margaret Smith) (1902-1971)

If there wasn't death, I think you couldn't go on.

Thomas Smollett (1721-1771)

Some folks are wise, and some are otherwise.

Sophocles (c. 496-406 B.C.)

Death is not the worst thing; rather, when one who craves death cannot attain even that wish.

Robert Southey (1774-1843)

Curses are like young chickens, they always come home to roost.

Your true lover of literature is never fastidious.

Scott Spendlove

If Abraham's son had been a teenager, it wouldn't have been a sacrifice.

Philip Dormer Stanhope, Fourth Earl of Chesterfield (1694-1773)

I recommend to you to take care of minutes, for hours will take care of themselves.

Advice is seldom welcome; and those who want it the most, always like it the least.

Elizabeth Cady Stanton (1815-1902)

The prolonged slavery of woman is the darkest page in human history.

Woman's discontent increases in exact proportion to her development.

Gertrude Stein (1874-1946)

We are always the same age inside.

There ain't no answer. There ain't going to be any answer. There never has been an answer. That's the answer.

Everybody gets so much information all day long that they lose their common sense.

John Steinbeck (1902-1968)

It would be absurd if we did not understand both angels and devils, since we invented them.

Gloria Steinem (1934-   )

The surest way to be alone is to get married.

I have yet to hear a man ask for advice on how to combine marriage and a career.

Stendhal (1783-1842)

All religions are founded on the fear of the many and the cleverness of the few.

Adlai Stevenson (1900-1965)

My definition of a free society is a society where it is safe to be unpopular.

A politician is a statesman who approaches every question with an open mouth.

Robert Louis Stevenson (1850-1894)

A little amateur painting in water-colours shows the innocent and quiet mind.

Politics is perhaps the only profession for which no preparation is thought necessary.

Everyone lives by selling something.

Bob Stokes (1958-   )

The world is proof that God is a committee.

Lionel Strachey (1864-1927)

The penalty for getting the woman you want is that you must keep her.

Jonathan Swift (1667-1745)

We have just enough religion to make us hate, but not enough to make us love one another.

Every man desires to live long, but no man would be old.

Michael Brooke Symons

Love is what makes the world go around – that and clichés.

Bert Leston Taylor (1866-1921)

A bore is a man who, when you ask him how he is, tells you.

Sara Teasdale (1884-1933)

No one worth possessing can be quite possessed.

Mother Teresa (Agnes Gonxha Bojaxhiu) (1910-1997)

I know God will not give me anything I can't handle. I just wish He didn't trust me so much.

Margaret Thatcher (1925-2013)

If you are going from A to B you do not always necessarily go in a straight line.

The battle for women's rights has been largely won.

Being powerful is like being a lady. If you have to tell people you are, you aren't.

Edward Thomas (1878-1917)

The past is the only dead thing that smells sweet.

Henry David Thoreau (1817-1862)

The mass of men lead lives of quiet desperation.

Beware of all enterprises that require new clothes.

Some circumstantial evidence is very strong, as when you find a trout in the milk.

Never look back unless you are planning to go that way.

Every generation laughs at the old fashions, but follows religiously the new.

Many men go fishing all of their lives without knowing it is not fish they are after.

Any fool can make a rule.

Lily Tomlin (1939-   )

The best mind-altering drug is truth.

No matter how cynical you get, it's impossible to keep up.

The trouble with being in the rat race is that even if you win, you're still a rat.

If truth is beauty, how come no one has their hair done in a library?

We 're all in this together...by ourselves.

We have reason to believe that man first walked upright to free his hands for masturbation.

It's my belief we developed language because of our deep inner need to complain.

When we talk to God, we're praying. When God talks to us, we're schizophrenic.

Jean Toomer (1894-1967)

The realization of ignorance is the first act of knowing.

Arnold Toynbee (1889-1975)

America is a large, friendly dog in a very small room. Every time it wags its tail it knocks over a chair.

Leon Trotsky (1879-1940)

Old age is the most unexpected of all the things that happen to a man.

Barbara Tuchman (1912-1989)

In the search for meaning we must not forget that the gods (or God, for that matter) are a concept of the human mind, they are the creatures of man, not vice versa…They exist to bear the burden of all things that cannot be comprehended except by supernatural intervention or design.

Martin Tupper (1810-1889)

Well-timed silence hath more eloquence than speech.

Mark Twain (Samuel Clemens) (1835-1910)

I have never let schooling interfere with my education.

Few things are harder to put up with than the annoyance of a good example.

Nothing so needs reforming as other people's habits.

A human being has a natural desire to have more of a good thing than he needs.

Everyone is a moon, and has a dark side which he never shows to anybody.

Many a small thing has been made large by the right kind of advertising.

We ought never do wrong when people are looking.

Man is the Religious Animal...He is the only animal that has the True Religion – several of them.

If the man doesn't believe as we do, we say he is a crank, and that settles it. I mean, it does nowadays, because now we can't burn him.

There is no distinctly American criminal class except Congress.

The less there is to justify a traditional custom the harder it is to get rid of it.

Age is an issue of mind over matter. If you don't mind, it doesn't matter.

Let someone else blow your horn and the sound will travel twice as far.

In all matters of opinion, our adversaries are insane.

Horace Annesley Vachell (1861-1955)

In nature there are no rewards or punishments; there are consequences.

Paul Valery (1871-1945)

An intelligent woman is a woman with whom we can be as stupid as we like.

Bill Vaughan (1915-1977)

A citizen of America will cross the ocean to fight for democracy, but won't cross the street to vote in a national election.

Felix Lope de Vega Carpio (1562-1635)

The most wise speech is not as holy as silence.

Gore Vidal (1925-2012)

Whenever a friend succeeds, a little something in me dies.

Never have children, only grandchildren

It is not enough to succeed. Others must fail.

Judith Viorst (1931-   )

A normal adolescent isn't a normal adolescent if he acts normal.

Voltaire (1694-1778)

Common sense is not so common.

If God has created us in his image, we have repaid him well.

If God did not exist, it would be necessary to invent him.

The earth swarms with people who are not worth talking to.

It is dangerous to be right when the government is wrong.

Kurt Vonnegut, Jr. (1922-2007)

True terror is to wake up one morning and discover that your high school class is running the country.

If you can do a half-assed job of anything, you're a one-eyed man in a kingdom of the blind.

We are what we pretend to be.

Izaak Walton (1593-1683)

No man can lose what he never had.

Booker T. Washington (1856-1915)

Few things help an individual more than to place responsibility upon him and to let him know that you trust him.

Martha Washington (1731-1802)

The greater part of our happiness or misery depends on our dispositions and not on our circumstances.

Lillian Eichler Watson (1902- c. 1975)

There has never been an age that did not applaud the past and lament the present.

James Watt (Secretary of the Interior) (1938-   )

We have every mixture you can have. I have a black, I have a woman, two Jews and a cripple.

J.C. Watts (1957-   )

Character is doing the right thing when nobody's looking.

Evelyn Waugh (1903-1966)

We cherish our friends not for their ability to amuse us, but for our ability to amuse them.

John Wayne (1907-1979)

Courage is being scared to death but saddling up anyway.

John Webster (c. 1580- c. 1625)

Cowardly dogs bark loudest.

A. H. Weiler (1908-2002)

Nothing is impossible for the man who doesn't have to do it himself.

H.G. Wells (1866-1946)

In the Country of the Blind the One-eyed Man is King.

Human history becomes more and more a race between education and catastrophe.

Dame Rebecca West (1892-1983)

God forbid that any book should be banned. The practice is as indefensible as infanticide.

There is no such thing as conversation. It is an illusion. There are intersecting monologues, that is all.

George Whitefield (1714-1770)

I had rather wear out than rust out.

Charlotte Whitton (1896-1975)

Whatever women do they must do twice as well as men to be thought half as good. Luckily, this is not difficult.

Oscar Wilde (1854-1900)

Life is too important to be taken seriously.

To be natural is a very difficult pose to keep up.

When the gods wish to punish us they answer our prayers.

A man can be happy with any woman as long as he does not love her.

In this world there are only two tragedies. One is not getting what one wants and the other is getting it.

Everybody who is incapable of learning has taken to teaching.

Education is an admirable thing, but it is well to remember from time to time that nothing that is worth knowing can be taught.

There is only one thing in the world worse than being talked about, and that is not being talked about.

A man cannot be too careful in the choice of his enemies.

The only way to get rid of a temptation is to yield to it.

I can resist everything except temptation.

Experience is the name every one gives to their mistakes.

In matters of grave importance, style, not sincerity, is the vital thing.

A thing is not necessarily true because a man dies for it.

Work is the curse of the drinking class.

Always forgive your enemies; nothing annoys them so much.

Some cause happiness wherever they go; others, whenever they go.

Religions die when they are proved true. Science is the record of dead religions.

A gentleman is one who never hurts anyone's feelings unintentionally.

Discontent is the first step in the progress of a man or a nation.

Nothing succeeds like excess.

Debt is the worst poverty.

Clerow "Flip" Wilson (1933-1998)

Violence is a tool of the ignorant.

Woodrow Wilson (1856-1924)

No one can worship God or love his neighbor on an empty stomach.

If you want to make enemies, try to change something.

Roger Woddis (1917-1993)

Men play the game; women know the score.

P.G. Wodehouse (1881-1975)

It is a good rule in life never to apologize. The right sort of people do not want apologies, and the wrong sort take a mean advantage of them.

Virginia Woolf (1882-1941)

Why are women...so much more interesting to men than men are to women?

If you do not tell the truth about yourself, you cannot tell it about other people.

T. Woolston

The Scriptures are full of incredibilities and absurdities.

Steven Wright (1955-   )

Why is the alphabet in that order? Is it because of that song?

When I turned two I was really anxious, because I'd doubled my age in a year. I thought, if this keeps up, by the time I'm six I'll be ninety.

Light travels faster than sound – isn't that why some people appear bright until you hear them speak?

I went to a restaurant that serves "breakfast at any time." So I ordered French Toast during the Renaissance.

You know when you put a stick in the water and it looks like it's bent but really isn't? That's why I don't take baths.

Sponges grow in the ocean...I wonder how much deeper the ocean would be if that didn't happen.

Xenophanes (c. 570-c. 480 B.C.)

Ethiopians say that their gods are snub-nosed and black, Thracians that theirs have light blue eyes and red hair.

Edward Young (1681-1765)

All men think all men mortal but themselves.

Procrastination is the thief of time.

Sources

Applewhite, Ashton, William R. Evans III, and Andrew Frothingham, eds. *And I Quote* New York: Thomas Dunne Books, 2003

Bradford, Gamaliel *Portrait of Margaret Fuller* **North American Review**

Byrne, Robert *The 2,548 Best Things Anybody Ever Said* New York: Simon & Schuster, 2006

Comayre, Gabriel Horace *Mann and the Public School in the United States* New York: Thomas Y. Crowell and Co., 1907

Grothe, Dr. Mardy *Oxymoronica: Paradoxical Wit and Wisdom from History's Greatest Wordsmiths* New York: HarperCollins, 2004

Jeffares, A. Norman, and Martin Gray, eds. *A Dictionary of Quotations* New York: HarperCollins, 1995

Jarski, Rosemarie *Dim Wit: The Stupidest Quotes of All Time* Berkeley: Ulysses Press, 2010

Lloyd, John, and John Mitchinson *If Ignorance is Bliss, Why Aren't There More Happy People: Smart Quotes for Dumb Times* New York: Harmony Books, 2008

Loeb, Aaron John, ed., *The Wit and Wisdom of Mark Twain* New York: Barnes and Noble Books, 1996

Petras, Ross and Kathryn *The 776 Stupidest Things Ever Said* New York: Doubleday, 1993

Smart Mouths: The Best Quotations Ever Collected Ashland, Oregon: Knowledge Commons

Sharma, Abhi *Best Quotes of All TimeSmat*

The New International Webster's Pocket Quotation Dictionary of the English Language Trident Press International, *2000*

The Quotable Woman Philadelphia: Running Press, 1991

ABOUT THE AUTHOR

Jerry Cavanaugh is a retired history teacher
currently living the good life in Florida.
His other works include *Illustrivia*, a series
of illustrated trivia books, and
From Cairo to Kazakhstan, a journal
of overseas teaching.